Edging

ISBN 0-9786440-0-X

First Edition

cover photo: Math Rod Garri

Cracked Slab Books
PO Box 378608
Chicago, IL 60637

http://www.crackedslabbooks.com

Edging

Michelle Noteboom

Cracked
Slab

Chicago 2006

Contents

Lost

There are doors and knocking. Try to open, if locked go under. Keep trying.
See, you are very small. Perhaps dirty. You do at times. Some people
whose flesh is crushed will do at times.

Odd thick words and looking in the sequined night. Sequins on a key. It filters
down like the mystery that is black, that is velvet. Mystery of looking.
Your breath, silken, condenses. A thumping noise.

Memory is still just an empty high in an odd valley lying supine on a blank
sheet. Long ago was letting go and forgetting. Remember only you
are being filled. Can barely see the key so far beyond.

In the desert, miles above, a tiny man with metallic flesh walks by the road.
In the middle of some nowhere, some she-thing emerges with broken
wings. A mangled surface. Touch it now, then awake.

In silence, an empty high being filled. Snakes twine the valley where low
lights glitter. Sequins on black velvet. Words crush the promise of looking.
Keep knocking.

To open the night keep knocking the doors of the netherworld, twist
and groan. Go under. The tiny man deceives you. He's lost his skin. Perhaps.
A steel-ribbed curtain clamps down.

On the curtain a delicate insect, a metal insect unfolds its silence. Its wings
are broken. They unlock. You are on the outskirts of something. Close. Stale
lives and seedy breathing. Something clicks.

I

The Edge

I.

You can press your fingers
in the troughs in my
flesh—hollow gouges
effected, modification,
art or healing, where
severed layers peel
back, are disposed of.
This is my body.
Chosen, chiseled,
its surface reworked,
reduced. Bits removed
to sate emptiness gnawing.

With a blunt knife shuck off
iridescent scales. Angling
a sharpened steel blade
at the throat, insert, work it
down the soft pale belly
to the vent. Viscera spills
easily away. In a series
of slicing movements
separate the flesh
from the rib cage. Above all,
disregard the lidless unseeing
lone eye beside your thumb.

This technique like
filleting—the upper tiers of
the dermis carved to create
a permanent design. It feels *strange*,
not quite *pain*. This isn't *bad*.
Crackling velcro release sensation.
The emptied space gapes
wider than the shrunken
swath it yields. Stroke the strip,
receive its warmth, satiny inside
of the body still alive
in the palm of your hand.

Waterborne

Through thick chemical medium, an infant when entering muggy yawn of wet sluicing damp air opening, my body muffled. Down myriad forms light dapples floating and scud-along color. Buoying cloudless chilly sensation fluent envelope upon first dip nor last. Plunging this grip in rippling through quenched. I the aqueous in amniotic love, that chance fluid warmth over face place. Racing limbs, sound moistens engulfing ears and distance. In basin all shades weightless and various speed. Slipped into shooting liquid sky. Along as I stroke. Will-never doesn't daunt be. Glide right off the wall into the mind.

The Edge

II.

What's surprising is her skin
with its bouquet of colors
changing daily, blooming, the part
which seems most alive in the
waxy sallow face and skull
yielding tufts of wispy hair—
deep rose encircling the eyes,
fuchsia under her nose where
the oxygen tube rubs, brown
and purple spots on frail
arms and legs, delicate flesh
of an overripe fruit going moldy.

There's a wooden statue
in the Burmese temple
on Jong Kham pond in Mae Hong Son
with a plaque—a saying
about life being a cycle
of "the old, illness and after that
get died. . .so what's
going on in the circle?" [sic]—
underneath the gaunt painted
figure mottled yellow and grey,
each rib sculpted sharp under
matte lacquer mimicking skin.

Mottling is a sign that death
is near. The heart sucks
oxygen from the extremities
where blood stops circulating
and pools. Purple blotches appear,
creep forth like roadmaps
developing along hands
and feet. This can last for
hours. When the heart finally
stops, the maps dissolve back
into the dermis which instantaneously
turns a rosy uniform pink.

4 p.m.

Far in my thoughts where cold sets in. Successful reality shoulders things not dreaming. Fade into lay and with it comes be. The pace of always creeping now, I and what will come. It's the ego trying to make hollow, find a way up into halt. Can feel all sorts of rings around this void. Clammy fingers encircling future days, melancholic when. Wander about to escape frightened. It follows me through my everything there. Some shivers here—the floors, windows, hours. I get nothing.

Experiment

Skin and gaze registered. Beyond, a rhythmic room where his receptors are laid, liquid, incidental, slowly rolling from side to side to pick up regularities. Diodes flash. I am struck by images which readily move into my hand: his features suspended in blood pausing, skull full of bulges, crustaceans on the back. The camera breathes his air, power of entrapment. Useless embryonic pain is fastened on my incandescent presence.

Step into being. In turn, nothing in his transmit corner. Use the cerebellum shadow translated thinly in pervasive light. I note his course or what my eyes have recorded. Lunar pull of abdominal pouch, pounded mud, his face. Astonishment or forearms with curious hair. An oscilloscope measures the sheer organic square, too human to adhere to exploratory studies. Diabolic object. Ascending filaments. Helpless willing blind subjects.

The reductions of retina are unique. Electrodes, diodes blink. I must have it out in a pattern. Information is then his living block of stimuli. During drainage, there is a lull in the brain. Moist surface of a matrix mounted on the plastic back of his body. Think 'crystal,' 'boiled vegetable,' designed with strength to deliver a person's head (its resilience). Suction or sticky transmitters of the normal.

Picked information is stored in the skin. I club one side and the eyes are enabled. Both cortex and panic converted to research. It is or has the consistency of an array of sensors. Incurvatures worn with an apparatus of graphs like unforgettable clothes. Barnacled torso. A camera wave pulses, drawn to his miner's lamp. Electrodes wink in tepid flesh to signal.

The Edge

III.

There's first a cool tickle
as the razor traces its lines,
maps the design, then a soft
zip, almost inaudible hissing
as skin parts, gives way
beneath the blade. The cut,
white at first, swiftly fills.
A sudden shiver, thin rivulets
of blood snake groundwards.
This is ritual, you think.
Beautiful. Satisfying.
The sweet chill icing the spine.

The notion of self is deeply
rooted in the sensorium. One
of the only places the mind
can sense the body is through
the skin, both a canvas
on which our personal & cultural
identity is drawn, and a battleground
where we struggle to define
boundaries of ourselves. Scalpels,
razors, scissors, knives & surgical tools
are arms in this ineffable war. Scars,
the mute signals of inner wounds.

He sits, rocks slightly,
reaching round to hug himself
in a sterile embrace. The movement
bares the pale smooth surface
of his upper arms—a latticework
of faint thin lines, razor-fine
interspersed with circular
purple spots where cigarettes
have pressed, singed, melted
flesh drawing forth pain
like poison sucked
from a snakebite.

II

The Edge

IV.

Something in the landscape
evokes the way color
and shade drape over swells,
fill hollows, envelop forms.
Your gaze follows the contours,
a caress. A woman
reclining in stillness, the mountains.
There's subtle movement like breathing.
Maybe your body has been
a maquette for the hills
You think of these lines, of earth
in its near invisible expansion.

Before the mirror she stands

naked to the waist gazing

at an unfamiliar unmapped zone.

Wary fingers trace the angry red ridge

stretching taut across a barren

plain, one hand explores

the absence, then glides

over to palm what is—what alone

looks peculiar. She cups

its form, holds its weight,

heavier now

than before.

One of the most remarkable things
about skin is its ability to stretch
& increase in surface area. Dr. Hilton
Becker invented the Becker Expander—
a silicone gel balloon surgically
implanted under muscle, inflated
by injections of saline. Within six
months the bag can double in volume.
New cells divide, migrate to fill
microscopic gaps as skin expands
3-4 times its original size, creating
a pocket for artificial tissue.

Exchange

City full of angels stroking their feet, women in pink in Bangkok.
The heading out for feel. One in ritual against my tension, sigh and
stare. Gentle hands know foreign thoughts, a silent body blessing.
Lay flat still trying to reach her language. Few words we share.
Closed eyes contain this spot where empty, two torsos of flesh and
bone dance. Coming from do as much as some void to palm this
prayer. Dynamics leave over, pull, walk round the globe. It's an
exchange line of energy dispelling any other commerce.
Uncomfortable though.

Covert

At 1 a.m. this man in the metro sitting. He was holding me and I noticed a bonsai. It was very dark, he was Indian and looked a Hindu prince, proud but ok. Fine features in natural elegant calm with very much beard. He was in black Jack London sweatshirt with miniature tree staring. Others interested curious they looking too. Then at Montparnasse young Americans got a group on. Loud laughing girls were puffed made-up pink. Drunken squeals dangling off Midwestern roots. Shut eyes I climbed the bonsai. From foreign tree my hidden face through tiny branches.

Cincture

Steeped in glass, a face stretching to
find me groping here, pressed.
I lay him and ask if it hurts,
knowing only what fingers see.

Finding me groped there, pressed in
a steel-spoked landscape clasp,
could he know he only sees fingers,
at midnight wears serpent eyes?

The steel spool of landscape rasps
inanely yanking the husk of
midnight. Weary serpent eyes scan
slopes & scales across a fleshy plain.

An inane yank and hush of
hands shuddering "yes please." Casting
scales & slopes into flesh of land,
sensing body pressure. My dark

shuttered hands. "Yes. Please cast."
Beyond us glistens the sweltering point.
Pressure of body-dark senses as
I chart out tears on the map

beyond listen. Weltering under
covers, dusk crushes in. He too
charters and tears at the map, keeps
eclipsing through physical pull.

Uncovering, dusk rushes over us
bending into crevice, breaking swell.
An eclipse, though physical, pulses and
encircles this wisp of a gaze.

Bending of crevice breaking, swell
steeped in glass. Face stretched to
cincture the want of his gaze as
we lay back to see if it hurts.

Fissure

Fluorescent interruption. Lips parched they part to impart what is left now the ineffable's been said, done, gone. You take my hand leading out. The body, a discontinuity, waiting for fog or motion. A costly risk we can't avoid. Silt settles at your feet, mine, undermining something below us that stays unduplicated. Bellowing fire, an alembic stem. Pretension of words amid combustion of leaving. Instead of asking for mercy we merely trace its shape. Mine is circular, a closed door. Cool clatter of dishes. Yours, hexagonal. Our liminal fingers etch out edges striped with longing, lingering there. Cells renew themselves, a horizontal urge surges then flows forth. A violet trickle we follow.

The Edge

V.

For the unseeing, vision is
carnal. A face, a midnight landscape
to be scaled, mapped, traced.
Hands assess the osseous frame,
structure the plain, smooth
bulbs & swells, moist
pebbles. Thumbs perceive sharp
outcroppings of brows, soft
globes below. Creases,
miniature crevices tell
age & character, erosions
of laughter or concern.

Like the retina, the skin's
sensory receptors enable
it to register stimuli,
convert patterns into images
in the cerebrum. Using electrodes
in an elastic matrix fixed
on the dermis, a camera mounted
on the blind person's head transmits
information to the body's surface
which in turn is relayed to
the brain. Abdominal skin
'sees' better than that of the back.

His whitewashed eyes hold
clouds of smoke,
fingers quiver like
moles' noses while they
root, grope their way through
perpetual night. A druid
drawn by telluric vibrations,
he locates pressure points,
follows energy lines which
crisscross the stretch of terrain
supine before him, he
pulls, rubs, kneads.

III

Beginnings

I was born on morning. Early big a word. Can't say 'soul' after 'country,' 'artery.' The emotional onset of native spirit. Viscera. Home a limb of land in which I've many. One can have. Was humid weather like anyone's? Linear gallic roads to cartesian here. U S anyway. Heavy text turning on the other. This stormy fiction a cut-up note. My disjointed shift. Capillary attraction. Now feel first life which won't explain 20 years of haven't-done. Biography. Wasted preparation of less thought. No buts, just a long _____

Patching for prelude to the real brain birth. My self implanted, a collage, right?

Cement

Brush of me and machinery in courtyards of remanent dreams. The nonchalant site smelled cool fresh aside. It was undeliberate newly poured action, was plaster damp chalky floors. All fairly if not completely devoid of any ill-gathered round intent like moths drawn blindly. The source of fawning a single-lit awe trailing sheer indifference. Cut quick. Was this but behind him, an object of room to room thinking in way of my presence? Words seem invisible: was I more solid?

Imagine

Haunting substantially below. To stop yet me. Today
your body felt real but discontinued. Rather faint share of
one, not. Urge like invented sentience.

Trembling

taste   fabricate

pointing now
however new
you

we long to

in order to

if only to

pure (reverie)

need for any truth
in,
and in,
and in,

some strange call

was that?

(make the bed)

the arch
nurtured, surrounded   knowing there

is
we

for so
long

ghostly and dim damp sounds on each tiny white hint

imagined

Chambers

Later that probing tabled and hashed daggers. At night to dream over what had. Sink into seemingly insurmountable become, would feel any anger at having. Couldn't fathom asking, tending mere solution of attention. Frustration stared at one sting welling back and anxious. Unmoved up in the verge of my heart over. Wanted bursting forth to hold back platters, humiliation. Not forthcoming so attacked. In kitchen threw icy steel sitting. At which point all sticking thoughts now central. Being. Another fear at ever going and tears on hands. Admit searching to draw you gently.

The Edge

VI.

At some primal level it is scent
that attracts (or repels) our mates:
skin cells progressing through
different stages of development
until they die, slough off in a
perpetual silent shower of debris.
2 to 3 billion cellular remnants shed
daily—enough from the foot alone
to add 190mg of dead cells to
a pair of socks. Each of us has
a genetically unique odor coded
into this skin that spills in our wake.

It wasn't the unfaithfulness

of the act that plagued

her—guilt could be reasoned

away—but rather

the condemning scent of another

wafting from her pores despite

hours of scouring, pumicing

her body raw, the razor scraping

each inch of flesh.

She couldn't bear smelling

like someone she was not. Taste

of sea swelling in her mouth.

A shining new scalpel lay on
the table, delicate thin, detachable
blades. "We'd been shedding clothes
all evening, scent of steel, triangle
of flesh. Fetish object." They spread her
out, brushed alcohol on her back,
blank canvas, began to cut. Could
feel burning in spite of cool
bursts of breath, sharp wet tongues.
"Later with a handmirror they
showed me the designs."
Star. Spiral. Pinwheel.

Grasp

A lie and then pull like sex in here. Though in truth illicit kisses toward you rest appropriate after thoughts, after courtyards. In bed next to easy, forget. Yet the images seem to know where to haunt me. Don't 'me'. Now see a scent slip into touch. Memory means nothing. Muscles can't still leaving (creeping thighs, you again all over). Most making betrays inconsiderately. Gasp across the bed whisper time. This man a temple. I know it when I'm lying. Hold back your taut flood, come to almost press your skin. Hard feeling unconsciously fingers such sturdy grasp onto me.

Eden

That night you collided, my voice belied frantic scorn because not whispering or waking or wanting. Attended to settling back into blankets of rage, we tore up sheets. Hissing. My eyes a live victim transuding disdain, fists burrowed a mattress of glistening. Venom and arms too stiff to move. On all fours you were a stranger kind of animosity rising. You wrenched sleepy urgency from under me standing on pillows of serpents and serpentine shapes. New tone entirely for one hundred cries, black corners of the bed writhing forth. An unspoken elbow of ulterior motion, clenched incomprehension in a universe of options at hand.

The Edge

VII.

The form of the disease
is as follows: spots, plaques,
avalanches of excess skin.
Above all the man looks
tired, his hollow gaze disseminates
no thing, he can't be *here*, really,
sitting on this metal bed in a
scant dhoti-like gown doused
with raw fluorescent light. Silvery,
scaly, puddles of flakes form
wherever he rests his flesh.
"Each morning I vacuum my bed."

A group of doctors cluster
like moths, scrutinizing,
scribbling notes, scraping his scabs.
"My classmates kept turning round
looking at me, whispering."
His silicious sheen, crusty
shell tends to shower down
like phosphorous or snow. Voices
low, they snap photos for future
reference, textbooks, case studies.
A black bar eclipsing
his blank stare.

So much white glare off coats
and tiles burns the retina.
Sterile click of shutter,
pen. Through some trifling but
persistent error in its metabolic
instructions, the dermis manufactures
a surplus of cells which expand,
slowly migrate across
the body like lichen on a
tombstone. "I'd close my eyes
as a child to try and hide,
but the body was always there."

Archeology

Clustered within surrounding soil, brittle intrusive jigsaw of organic measurements and informed fractal space. Technicians employ magnetic plaster rods & sequences to prepare cells. They stare through electron microscopes at life-sized binding forces, as if disentangling the future could enable a breathing creature, undertaking a complete organism of flesh only to unfold it in a semi-virtual zone. They use interstitial identification to refill cracks in extracted earthen boxes, excavate spinal implants and lay each piece on the skin like jewelry. Clay, melded mechanical organs, bionic malfunctions in computerized constructs.

The hominid of emergence burgeons forth from the loam. Biotic figures reconstituted, metal body bits in a united dwelling space beyond epoxy form. Androgynous underneath and ghostly confident, wearing optical implants to eye across time.

Fixation

Me out fetched of the drive that rainy
Saturday and bandages. Grow supine to settle
in cozy chrome litanies of difference scattered
throughout veins. Tangle of blazing and
blades.

The chassis stretched delicate across
the wounds, sexual potential in its own surge
of power. Time more romantic without ever
grazing a swirl.

In the shed red honeysuckle
now wound round each other. Metallic
geometry of breath as we opt for caress.
Alcohol rush in living exchange. Innocent
clothing on the back of a cotton sensation.
Being.

Fragile. Limbs bound to spite throttle
of night, sever or enable someone else. Damp
tongued flesh. Multiple blows in reciprocal
passion too shy to tell.

Laps wrapped tight in our
trust carving snug under blanketed lips. Shift
into scent of me straddled.

IV

Chafed

In the stylized abstract chess I was the checkered queen.

By sequined greeting atmosphere beckoning, token to the new entrance and evening game with several. The marbled nymphs in wigs to scandalize right through the recondite arcade, stepping to a hellish realm of players clad in townhouse-flanked orangish art. Organs.

A heady door.

Taking a hungered lure through the techno throb-plastified feast, full moon rising on their heels. A real princess, her bleached busted form.

Tossed round the honeyed make, I was right-fingered fashioned spread out on the overly-bare haunches, reigning in a fleecy crop of pawns and prize. Hardened lurid becoming. A gold-earned kiss
and entrails. . .

Chrysalis

Ask always which gaze direction objects shouldn't be. A chair hints the world that lies outside of humans. We = a privilege. Intimacy. Fringing the escarpment, the scarab presence for purposed articulation, stable grinding over of. Absence. The grammar is olfactory. Wind in the wickered shimmering of tiny mandibles, all the cameras, a mosquito. A living place that never was so cold. Understanding is a question of frame or fire. Sitting in an empty chair, a boy is a visual engagement richer than insects, is infinitely frayed though entertained. Beyond want-to-be and exoskeletons, this fake city built on the ruins of a former hum. He comes carrying to distract. The silvery-winged threshold of hallucination and lace, yet a thousand bodies bear the weight. Yellowed light and ash, to swallow.

The Model

just so much flesh folded
in upon itself to be
decomposed

Object :

eyes all observing roaming roving scanning mapping capting measuring
scaling slopes & bulges   prying hollows & arcs
circumscribing the whole
plying each centimeter of surface

hands all mirroring motion mimicking movement of eye
in out thumbing cupping curving cusping pinching palming earth
coaxing a lump   whittling a scrape
wrist calf elbow ankle knee collarbone rib

one solid mass slightly breathing
        (her eyes her freedom following
        fingers fondling counterfeit breasts and vulvas
        fashioned on her own

        (passive witness to. . .

intimate acts
carnal knowledge
          through observation

the rub nudge smooth stroke thrust of it

Subject :

translate the attack isn't the yield and bend
bone and flesh was something of a tiny
likeness though surrogate self almost all
assessed exhibitionist aspect of a thigh or
mold looking at smoothing back gazes in
and upper press glide down each grapple
once wresting essence from nipples now
teased and transmuted through instruments
of capture nor assault there where clay
watching them dip and delve one by one
eyes running saw digging with picks and
curious hands curving out hips to meet
their

me

not me

each physical body

it was the measurement

working articulation
giving living form
seeking alteration or

                    release

where kneading fingers strive secret under touch

Back

At dusk my us unable to father sleep in a tight in a plastic still uncontrollable sheet, a cocoon, to rip a hole near impossibility in his mouth, prevent begging for such anxious. Night always confused at these. Drive me to my bearings, all-American lie lost now, the only sure nullified. Like things that get far away and bewildered back to European ground. Three times last again, that dream hammock wrapped being stuck in same nightmare of I, tore frantically for some reason, catch the plane or him suffocating circumstances. Wake in a sweat. Hurry! Changing surroundings. Make it to know where am, to perpetual and then doomed. Push out and relate freedoms. Choose life or.

Choice/Choler

There's this encephalic us as we masticate, sit smiting open to homogenize so little. With because am. When & what raft is the air shaft or e-scape, is a finite period? Couldn't legitimate this knowing that. You said silence on the way before time mouthed worth in. Wondering fills hours ago. Some technique. Can't why I the gun-shy one, so eccrine I cling to your glittering. Goodbye a beginning, fermenting in unfeathered depths. Form legislates life. Months own of an end then tell unspoken airless behind.

morning

      after   under

comfort of hours a long flow
let over. heat moving in watery
envelope
mouth taste of wine. traces of smoke
all down the thickness
drunk throbbing for whole.
gone.
chilly luxury of got-nothing-
much. feelings turn in—out. head full
with water. lying still bare cotton
sipping staves moving in woolen
midnight
shroud. music warms husk off the room.
today drains now makes way
through empty flat to shower
me where I stand.

Chafed

. . .A table set

        where tufts, stiletto drapery of white, instant drones flocking bodies on the ring. Just the pout and salty hair. The brief reward was confirmed with swaddled instruments of painting, a vulgar take behind the chocolated cellar.

Later the fleshy lips and foundling, merited desire redolent to the breast, a subgenre-d baccanal thing barreled in the brew. It took hours. Welling innocence clutched amidst a rendition of some sprawled-over decision in a taxi. Images flickering breathless on the wall.

Shift the course. Culmination

        in a commodity and my thighs.
Sudden neon u-turn night in grace-misted sticky sour question. Barely-booted streets. Near crashing fall. What price, took worth.

The sweet instant curdled, untaken. Drafting deflation, residue unclung. My black deserted cobblestone.

The Edge

VIII.

As he moves, mouths flicker,
eyes wink. If you close yours,
stroke his body, you can't feel
the ebb and flow of
glittering pictures, glowing
charcoals, a simmering riot
of rockets and events, intricate
designs mirroring what
is to be: crystal ball
inscribed in the flesh
of the Illustrated Man.
The fate of all he meets.

She wore only a seven-inch
Bengal tiger on Interstate 80.
New Jersey, 1991. Cat crouched
taut, creeping down her thigh,
stalking some unseen prey.
Rough-hewn work of an amateur.
In terms of forensics
such a mark, indelibly deep,
usually provides distinctive
means of ID
even after the body
begins to decompose.

Tokyo University displays
an army of headless figures,
synthetic forms with shortened
limbs, each sheathed in a garment
its wearer chose to shed
at his death. They stand
in glass cabinets unbreathing,
uninhabited wetsuits aswirl
with chrysanthemums, carp, dragons,
a samurai with a sword
clenched in his teeth. *Meiji period.*
Anonymous. Ink on skin.

Epilogue

Our bodies are becoming a new kind of language. We have at last reached the isotonic point and shall soon transcend the proscenium arch. Bifurcation or obfuscation? This remains to be seen.

Insatiable strategies sprawl down cavities of skin into a self-calibrating environment of possibility. Strings of ones and zeros unfurl across the tabular sky in a slow constant dissolve. Time sheds its liminal shell to join the insect-like creatures plying the ephemeral mainframe. Our respective transgressions trail its murky wake.

If you consider the migration patterns in the substrates of the oldest codes, the world starts to appear simply as multidimensional scaling. The mouths at the breast of the network whisper of transition. The question now on everyone's lips: "why not dig up through the green light?"

We continue daily leveling the structures, though the bandwidth seems to be unraveling. The surface tooling hints at analog lines. Imagine. Yet it would be an error to neglect the stratigraphical evidence hollow-cast in the soil-stained shoal. At the very least, it could serve as an alternative to edging.

Notes

Much of the work in this manuscript grew out of an obsession with skin and body that began in December 2001. Manyl things in my life seemed to converge in a way to get me thinking about these issues in new and different ways. Several of the poems in this collection, and in particular *The Edge* series, were inspired and informed by much of the reading and research I did at the time. Among the many books, magazines, articles and websites I came across, I would like to cite the following for their importance to the series:

Arthur Balin and Loretta Pratt Balin: The Life of the Skin (Bantam, 1997).

Marc Lappé: The Body's Edge (H. Holt, 1996), in particular for the middle section of *The Edge (III)*.

Ashley Montagu: Touching: The Human Significance of the Skin (Columbia University Press, 1971), in particular for the middle section of *The Edge (V)*.

Kathrin Perutz: Beyond the Looking Glass: America's Beauty Culture (Morrow, 1970).

And the website www.bme.freeq.com.

The Edge (II) is dedicated to my grandmother.

The Edge (III) is dedicated to my brother.

The first section of *The Edge (IV)* contains a slight variation of lines from Carol Snow's *Positions of the Body VI* in For (University of California Press, 2000).

The Edge (VII) is based on and borrows from John Updike's short story "From the Diary of a Leper."

The first section of *The Edge (VIII)* refers to Ray Bradbury's eponymous character in the novel The Illustrated Man. The facts about the tiger woman in the second section come from The Total Tattoo Book (Warner Books, 1994) by Amy Krakow.

Fissure comes from a project entitled "The Midnight Poems," a collaborative experiment with Barbara Beck, Jennifer K. Dick and Lisa Pasold which took place in January and June 2003.

The epilogue is adapted out of "The Chia Letters" which appeared in The Moosehead Anthology X (edited by Todd Swift, DC Books, 2005), a series inspired largely by a blend of William Gibson, *National Geographic* and *Scientific American*. I would also like to cite From Black Land to

<u>Fifth Sun: The Science of Sacred Sites</u> (Helix Books, 1999) by Brian Fagan as proving crucial to the series.

Acknowledgements

Grateful acknowledgement is made to the editors the editors of the following journals, anthologies, and on-line publications in which these poems (sometimes in different versions and with different titles) first appeared:

Aufgabe: Exchange, Back
Boston Review: Lost
Diner: Eden
Gargoyle: Experiment
The Moosehead Anthology X: Epilogue
nthposition: Archeology
Pharos (France): Chambers
Salt Hill: The Edge VI
Short Fuse Global Anthology of New Fusion Poetry: Covert, Grasp.
Tears in the Fence (UK): Beginnings
Upstairs at Duroc (France): Imagine, Grasp

Many thanks to Mary Jo Bang, Barbara Beck, Jennifer K. Dick, Lisa Pasold, Sarah Riggs, Joe Ross, Rod Smith, Todd Swift, and George Vance for their guidance, support, advice, and insightful readings of this work.

Author's Biography

Michelle Noteboom was born and raised in Grand Rapids, Michigan. After completing a BA from the University of Michigan in 1991, she moved to Paris where she continued her education at the Sorbonne, completing a French Master's degree. Michelle co-curates the Paris-based Ivy Writers Reading Series along with Jennifer K. Dick and also translates French poetry. Her poems have appeared or are forthcoming in publications such as *Columbia Poetry Review, Verse, Fence* and *Sentence*. She works as a freelance translator primarily in the French audiovisual field and currently splits her residency between Paris and Michigan.

author's photo: Jennifer Huxta

Current and Forthcoming Books by Cracked Slab Books

Edging, Michelle Noteboom.
Thirty Chicago Poets, Eds. Raymond Bianchi and William
        Allegrezza.
Levitations, Garin Cycholl.

Cracked Slab Books would like to acknowledge the aid and
advice of George Compiani in the preparation of this book.
We also would like to thank Waltraud Haas and Lori Ryan.

Cracked Slab

Cracked Slab Books was started to provide an outlet for experimental poetry and mixed media works. With the aim of publishing at least two books a year, Cracked Slab Books is dedicated to promoting new American writers and to introducing the English-speaking world to interesting international poetry and mixed media work.

Editor: William Allegrezza
Publisher: Raymond Bianchi

For more information, please visit our web site:
http://www.crackedslabbooks.com

Cracked Slab Books
PO Box 378608
Chicago, IL 60637
USA